YOUR KNOWLEDGE HAS VALUE

Bibliographic information published by the German National Library:

The German National Library lists this publication in the National Bibliography; detailed bibliographic data are available on the Internet at http://dnb.dnb.de .

Imprint:

Copyright © 2016 GRIN Verlag
Print and binding: Books on Demand GmbH, Norderstedt Germany
ISBN: 9783346030917

This book at GRIN:

https://www.grin.com/document/499555

Shah Niaz

Soft skills and their effects on software project management

GRIN Verlag

GRIN - Your knowledge has value

Since its foundation in 1998, GRIN has specialized in publishing academic texts by students, college teachers and other academics as e-book and printed book. The website www.grin.com is an ideal platform for presenting term papers, final papers, scientific essays, dissertations and specialist books.

Visit us on the internet:

http://www.grin.com/

http://www.facebook.com/grincom

http://www.twitter.com/grin_com

Soft Skills and their Effects on SPM

Shah Niaz Khan

Riphah International University

I. INTRODUCTION

The software industry moves too fast toward new methods for managing the ever-increasing complexity of software projects. In the past years we have seen evolution, revolutions and recurring themes of success and failure of software projects .While software technologies, processes and methods have advanced rapidly, software engineering remains a people intensive process. Consequently, controlling the resources and techniques for managing people, technology and risks also have a big impact on the software projects. To manage all the activities in a software project the software industry introduced the course of software project management which is the art and science of planning, scope management and leading the software projects. It is a sub-discipline of project management in which software projects are planned, implemented, monitored and controlled. (1) In the software project management different types of stakeholders are involved. Everyone has its own responsibility and work according to the domain These stakeholders consist of project managers, business analysts, development team, QA team and end users etc. All the stakeholders have some abilities and skills which consist of technical skills or hard skills and some of them are soft skills. These skills are very necessary especially for project managers and the development team and also for quality assurance team that will work onward on the project. The development teams, on the other hand, also have to be master in both type of skills either hard skills (technical skills) or soft skills. Hard skills are the technical skills within the domain of the project we are managing. If we are managing a bridge building project, we must understand something about bridge building. If we are managing a semiconductor development project, we must understand something about semiconductor development, or the skills of requirement gathering, planning, design, coding, testing, or creating Gantt charts, conducting status meeting, calculation and 'many others are known as Hard skills but to realize the value of those hard skills requires soft skills such as communication skills, Negotiating skills, Leading Teams, Coaching, Motivating and a lot of other skills. Investing time and energy to improve soft skills is an investment in ourselves that will help us and our stakeholders to better realize the value of our hard skills.(2) soft skills are all about human factor and the experience of the skilled project manager and the development team which are crucial to providing the glue for the entire team to work and perform together. If a company have the best tools, systems and the processes but the people do not manage to work together then the company is in for failure.(3)Our task was to perform a detailed analysis of the soft skills , their identification and their effects on SPM. In this paper we present the result of our study to identify all of the human factor skills or soft skills. This paper is organized as follows. Section 1 is based on the introduction of the problem and a brief knowledge of project management and skills. Section 2 is about the identification of different stakeholders and their roles. Section 3 is based on the detail note on soft skills and on their importance. Section 4 is describe a case study. Section 5 is based on the comparative discussion . Section 6 is based on the proposed solution. Section 7 describes the conclusion and observation and gives a brief result of this research.

II. STAKEHOLDERS OF A PROJECT

Identifying your project stakeholders is the key to your project's success. Stakeholders can champion your project and help drive success, but they can also be very effective saboteurs. Powerful stakeholders are much more likely to sabotage your project if they don't feel engaged. The figure below should you to identify your project stakeholders. (4)

Figure 1: Analysis of project stakeholders.
[Source http://www.stakeholdermap.com/project-stakeholders.html][4]

Figure 1 shows different stakeholders of a project

that can be effect our project or can be a part of it. Here we will discuss some of them and their roles.

A. PROJECT MANAGER

The person responsible for the delivery of the project to time, cost and quality/scope. Likely to be the person responsible for identifying the project stakeholders. There may be more than one project manager on larger projects &programs.

B. PROJECT TEAM

The team who will deliver your project. They may be a virtual team assembled specifically for your project and they may be working on the project full or part-time. Without them project won't happen.

C. USERS

Users may or may not form part of your project team, but they will be impacted by the project deliverables. They will contribute requirements, & may be involved in testing, training, piloting, marketing, post-project reviews and so on. User feedback positive and negative will find its way to senior management either directly or indirectly.

D. QUALITY MANAGEMENT TEAM

The project deliverables will be measured against specific quality criteria. Assessments may be carried out by a specialist function or to a quality management system. Look for quality or test teams and bear in mind that multiple teams/functions may be involved.

III. SOFT SKILLS

In this paper we will be looking at some of the most important soft skills that are essential and important especially for the project manager and the other team. It has long been recognized that screening for and developing nontechnical "soft" skills in project managers and other employees is critical for the continued success of any complex, fast-changing organization. Such skills correspond primarily to A Guide to the Project Management Body of Knowledge (PMBOK® Guide) (PMI, 2004)

Knowledge Area entitled Human Resource Management, and secondarily to the Communications Management Knowledge Area. The general management literature indicates the importance of leadership and other such "soft" skills in management of organizations and in improving efficiency and output, as well as the importance of teamwork and the ability of a manager to create an environment in which the team can flourish.(5)One technology company anecdotally indicates that 90–95% of its documented performance issues annually are concerned with such "soft" skills as leadership, teamwork, management, and communication, with only the remaining 5–10% concerned with an employee's technical knowledge or ability. (5) Here we discuss some of these important skills .which are Communication skills, Negotiating skills, Leadership, Coaching, Decision making and management etc.

A. COMMUNICATION

Communication skills refer to the ability to convey ideas easily and clearly in order to ensure that the team moves towards a common goal. It is the very important soft skill for the project managers to communicate effectively today communication skills come in many different flavours, and the technical part certainly plays an important role here as well. First of all when dealing with people there is Body language. (3) These are aspects you can control, and you can influence on purpose, such as your gesture, standing up, or sitting down. Crossing your arms or reaching out a hand, which may influence the way the person in front of you interacts and feels at ease. When you have started conversationmake sure you use the right words; the right wordings is often very important. If you are working in a special domain, make sure you are familiar with all the acronyms used in the technical papers about the topic. And make sure your questioning reflects this. Then there are the listening skills. This is equally very important. You can try and obtain information from your speaker in a supportive, helpful way. Or there is the analyzing way, where you are trying to disentangle facts from emotions. And a third way is to synthesize while you are listening, and guide the conversation toward an objective you want to obtain.(3)Effective and to the point communication is essential. This should be carefully planned as part of your communications plan. Effective means that the message that is expected by the receiver will of course be part of what will be delivered. If it is not, you will fail and disappoint the opposite party. Also the timing of communication should be respected, and the media these days can be of importance as well.

B. NEGOTIATING

The second important soft skill is NEGOTIATING. Successful negotiating, an attempt by two parties to achieve a mutually acceptable solution, should not result in a winner and a loser. Both parties should be prepared to give in somewhat to achieve their goals. The art of negotiation is based on attempting to reconcile what constitutes a good result for you with what constitutes a good result for the other party. Some basic skills you will need to negotiate include the ability to define a range of objectives, the ability to explore a wide range of options, and the ability to prepare well. You should be able to listen and question other parties, and you should be able to prioritize clearly.(3)

Key Points:

When preparing for negotiating deals, these tips may be useful:
- ➢ It is impossible to do too much preparation
- ➢ Be prepared to compromise when you negotiate
- ➢ Write down all your objectives; then rank them
- ➢ Which issues are open to compromise and which are not?
- ➢ Begin with general uncontroversial points
- ➢ Wait for the other party to finish before responding

> Offer small concessions first — you may not need to go any further

C. LEADERSHIP

According to Dobbins and Pettman (1997), "leadership is the ability to motivate people to work towards achieving common goals, to make ordinary people display extraordinary performance." Leadership is one of the main functionality of the software project manager that he should always lead from the front. A software project manager should be someone whom people want to seek out rather than avoid (Bruce & Langdon, 2000). According to Bruce & Langdon (2000), four leadership styles (Dictatorial, Analytic, and Opinion-seeking, Democratic) may be associated with software project managers. It is essential to understand how teams work, and what the characteristics of a good team are. A true team is a living, constantly changing dynamic force in which a number of people come together to work. The team discusses their objectives, assesses ideas, makes decisions, and works together toward their targets. The leader should create a good atmosphere in which everybody can express his or her ideas and contribute to the goals to achieve. The leader is there only to facilitate this atmosphere, and inspire his or her team, and make sure the tasks are implemented in a coordinated fashion.

D. COACHING AND MENTORING

Coaching and mentoring use the same skills and approach, but coaching is a short-term task-based and mentoring is a longer term relationship. We can see coaching as a logical extension of training. Training is required to teach the trainee something new: an activity, a process, a procedure, a way of working, and so forth. It is theory based and stuffed with examples. The training can include some practical exercises but these are often limited in time and specifically chosen to demonstrate the new things. (3)
Some tips for effectively coaching include:
> Train your people so they can undertake a variety of tasks

> Set an example to your staff by being trained yourself
> Follow up regularly when delegating (weekly)

E. MOTIVATION

Motivation is the next Soft skill. Today's increasingly competitive business world means that a highly motivated workforce is vital for any organization. Therefore, learning how to motivate others has become an essential skill for managers. We will look here at how to put theories into practice to create and sustain a positive environment.

F. DECISION-MAKING

Decisions are an essential part of life, in and out of the work environment. Decision makers are those who are responsible for making a judgment – sometimes a crucial judgment – between two or more alternatives. First of all, decisions can usually be categorized as routine, emergency, strategic, and operational. Based on the type, you may have different sets of criteria to judge your decision, or the ways of analyzing your options may vary.(3)

G. TEAM BUILDING

The software project manager should be able to set up a team with an appropriate mix of skills to ensure the successful completion of a project.

H. FLEXIBILITY AND CREATIVITY

Flexibility and creativity can be promoted through the understanding of the personality of individual members, and acceptance of individual preferences (16).The software project manager should appreciate the abilities of the each team member and the belief that each and every individual is perfectible. The software project manager should provide opportunities to the team members to initiate actions and encourage creativity.

I. Stress management

Stress refers to pressure, tension or worry resulting from problems (8). Stress management is necessary for the software project manager. A certain level of stress is important for the software project manager to perform well and this type of stress is called eustress, which is good stress(7). When stress becomes excessive, it can cause harm to oneself or to the immediate surroundings. Beyond a certain level, it can cause distress(7).Distress is also harmful because it can lead to different problems like (physical problems, emotional problems, mental problems and behavioral problems)which may affect the health of someone and at the same time it may affect the progress of the project.

J.   CHANGE MANAGEMENT

Changes management is the very important task for the software project managers because the new developments in technology are brought about continually. If some change are required in the product than the project manager should reschedule the task and estimation will be done again to save the project from failure and gain the tasks within the budget and time.

K. TRUSTWORTHINESS

Trustworthiness is the value given to the belief that one can rely on the goodness, strength and ability of someone else (8). Mutual trust must prevail throughout the project execution between the software project manager and all of the stakeholders involved in the project. Simply meeting deadlines is just one facet of the objectives of a project; a software project manager must also be able to convey that he/she can always be trusted to do what is right at the right time to render the project successful and the client satisfied (12).

IV. A CASE STUDY

As part of our study, we study the analysis of 2000 IT advertisements collected and analyzed during the first half of August 2012. From the analysis of these soft skills found in these advertisements the((Ilana and Aharon.2013)) produced a list of required twenty skills. They further classified these soft skills into four main categories; The human interaction skills (high on the demand list) which includes the skills need to interact with other people (i.e.

employees, customers, peers, etc.), The common or general skills were in second place. The interaction skills are on third placed which includes the skills that are necessary for working in a computerized environments and performing the required tasks, The organization interaction skills are place on fourth place(the least requested) which includes the skills that are needed for proper functioning in the organization.

TABLE II: CATEGORIZED CLASSIFICATIONS

Human interaction skills	Task interaction skills	Organization interaction skills	Common (or general) skills
Team player	Can-do attitude	Work under pressure	Independent
Human relations	Analytical	Multi - tasking	Flexible
Presentations	Organized	Business oriented	Focused
Service oriented	Self-learner	Systemic /holistic	Highly motivated
Expressive			Creative
Instructor			Initiator/promoter

Figure 2: Classification of skills.
[Source http://www.ijeeee.org/Papers/270-CZ501.pdf][18]

Thus they have categorized these skills according to the emerging categories.

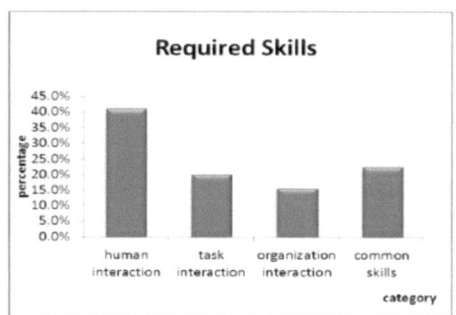

Figure 3: Distribution of skills according to the emerged categories.
[Sourcehttp://www.ijeeee.org/Papers/270-CZ501.pdf][18]

V. COMPARATIVE STUDY

We have conducted a literature review of past research and studies based on the soft skills .In our literature review we have collect 10 papers that describes soft skills and their effectiveness on project management. We have conclude their identification and results in the table below that represents authors name and their work.

Papers → / Soft Skills ↓	Kris Troukens 2015	Edward Muzio et al 2007	Jim De Piante 2010	Sharlett Gillard 2009	Vijay K. Verma, 1995	Ira Pant, Bassam Baroudi 2007	Aneerv et al. 2005	Steven 2015	Ilana and Aharon 2013	Mark et al. 2013
Communication	✓	✓		✓	✓	✓	✓	✓	✓	✓
Negotiation	✓		✓					✓		✓
Leadership	✓	✓	✓		✓	✓	✓		✓	✓
Coaching	✓		✓		✓	✓	✓			✓
Motivation	✓	✓		✓		✓	✓		✓	✓
Decision Making	✓	✓			✓		✓		✓	✓
Time Management	✓	✓			✓	✓	✓			✓
Responsibility			✓	✓	✓				✓	✓
Conflict management		✓				✓	✓	✓		✓
Team building			✓			✓	✓		✓	✓
Stress Management	✓				✓		✓		✓	✓
Organizational Effectiveness	✓	✓			✓		✓		✓	✓
Change management		✓					✓			✓
Trustworthiness								✓		✓
Flexibility and creativity	✓						✓		✓	✓

VI. PROPOSED SOLUTION

From our literature review of above 10 papers and after their comparative study come to the point that the soft skills are the key to success for the software project manager and for the other stakeholders. The foundation of soft skill or the essential skill is Communication. The PMI [19] suggest that a project manager should spend 90 percent of their time on communication because about one out five projects fail due to ineffective communication. Improvement in the communication begins with the success of each interaction. The communication mechanism and suggestions can help us mastering the soft skills and understanding the problems such as photographs, drawings, sounds and gestures.

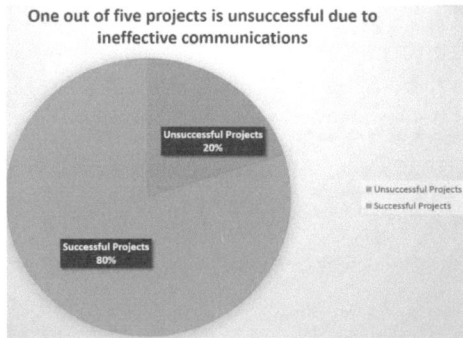

One out of five projects is unsuccessful due to ineffective communications

Source: ©2013 Project Management Institute, Inc. Pulse of the Profession In-Depth Report: The High Cost of Low Performance: The Essential Role of Communications May 2013. PMI.org/Pulse

VII. CONCLUSION

In software project management the technical and non-technical both skills are very important for the project manager and other team members to complete the project according to budget, schedule and technical specifications. If the organization has the best tools, systems and processes but if the project manager does not manage the team members to work together then project will fail. According to our study and One technology company indicates that "90–95% of its documented performance issues annually are concerned with such "soft" skills as leadership, teamwork, management, and communication, with only the remaining 5–10% concerned with an employee's technical knowledge or ability"[20]. The soft skill are not only necessary for the project managers but also important for the other employees as well. Today gradually changes are taking place in the field of technology leadership and practice. As the projects are going to increase in size and become complex then it is the need of the technical professional to develop competencies in people skills. These people skills can be well defined, practiced, and continuously improved by experience (through formal and informal workshops, meetings or executive coaching).

From the above study and the research based on the past work finally we came to know that soft skills are the main part of the success that need more improvement and practices. Although we have identify hundreds of soft skills that are necessary for the project manager and for the other stakeholders but we have selected some important skills which play a vital role in the project management process and can help us to make succeed our project according to our desired goals. These skills are effective leadership, problem solving and decision making, effective communication, sound work habits, ability to persuade and ability to resolve conflict. According to our proposed solution if we improve our communication skills that is very necessary for anyone who is involved in the software project management process like project manager, development team, quality assurance, designing etc. then we can convey our ideas to the opponent and can respond to them effectively. Software development process needs more attention and improvement in communication because it is very necessary to understand the requirement of a customer and forward their ideas to development team and make it possible that they have completely understand it so they can continue their work according to the customer or client needs and achieving the desired goals because almost 80 percent project succeeded due to effective to communication. We can justify our results in two categories first for the process and other employees that they must have the specified soft skills and the Secondly, the project manager if he not successful in identifying specific strong and weak skill areas for individual employees. The project manager was particularly blind to the strengths of weaker performers and the weaknesses of stronger performers, both of which are essential for employee and software development. In short we can say that Soft skills are extremely important for any project manager and for the others to obtain the desired results. This research paper should put the organization on right track to make their success.

VIII. REFERENCES

[1] Software Project Management, Wikipedia [online]

available:

http://en.wikipedia.org/wiki/ Software Project Management

[retrieved: November, 2015].

[2] The Soft Part is The Hard Part[Research Paper]

available:

http://www.pmi.org/learning/communicate-clearly-effectively-soft-skills-6621
retrieved: November, 2015].

[3] Sharpen your Soft Skills in this Workshop of Underestimated Project Management Tool.: [online]

By Kris Troukens,PMP

available:

http://www.pmi.org/learning/skills-underestimated-project-management-tools-5918

[retrieved: November, 2015].

[4] Analysis of project stakeholders [online]

available:

http://www.stakeholdermap.com/project-stakeholders.html

[retrieved: November, 2015].

[5] Soft skill quantification [online] [paper]

available:http://www.pmi.org/learning/soft-skills-quantification-predicting-performance-5638

[retrieved: November, 2015].

[6] Belzer, K. (2004). Project management: Still more art than science. Retrieved August 19, 2004, from

http://www.pmforum.org/library/papers/BusinessSuccess.htm

[7]: AneeravSukhoo, Andries Barnard, Mariki M. Eloff, John A. Van der Poll.2005" Accommodating Soft Skills in Software Project Management"." Issues in Informing Science and Information Technology"

(Aneeravet al.2005)

[8] Oxford Advanced Learner's Dictionary. (1999).

[9] Dobbins, R. &Pettman, B. O. (1997). Self-development: the nine basic skills for business success. Journal

of management development, 16(8), 521.

[10] Bruce A. & Langdon, K. (2000): Project management. New York: Dorling Kindersley.

[11] Fowdar, R. R. R., Peerally, J. A., Boolaky, M., Baichoo, R., Lai Wah, D., Gokhool, D., Vencatachellum, I.,

&Seebaluck, A. (2004). Organisation and management. Course manual. University of Mauritius.

[12] Lussier, R.N. (1990). Human relations in organisations. Homewood, IL: Irwin.

[13]: IlanaLavy and Aharon Yadin.2013." Soft Skills – An Important Key for Employability in the "Shift to a Service Driven Economy" Era". International Journal of e-Education, e-Business, e-Management and e-Learning 2013.

(Ilana and Aharon.2013)

[14]: Mark Keil, Hyung Koo Lee ,Tianjie Deng 2013." Understanding the most critical skills for managing IT projects: A Delphi study of IT project managers". Information & Management.

(Mark et al.2013)

[15]:StevenFlannes 2015." Effective People Skills for the Project Manager: A Requirement for Project Success and Career Advancement", Planning, Development and Support.

(Steven 2015)

www.2.sas.com/proceedings/sugi29/131-29.pdf

[16]Santrock, J. W. (2000). Psychology (6th ed.). Congress Lib.

[18] Soft Skills – An Important Key for Employability in the "Shift to a Service Driven Economy" Era
http://www.ijeeee.org/Papers/270-CZ501.pdf
[retrieved: November, 2015].

[19]http://2020projectmanagement.com/2014/06/communication-the-key-to-successful-project-management/

[20] Behavioral Technology. (1999). Behavioral interviewing participant manual. Behavioral Technology®, Inc.

YOUR KNOWLEDGE HAS VALUE

.